Fertile Decay

Glory Cumbow

Parson's Porch Books

Fertile Decay
ISBN: Softcover 978-1-955581-53-0
Copyright © 2022 by Glory Cumbow

Parson's Porch Books is an imprint of Parson's Porch *&* Company (PP*&*C) in Cleveland, Tennessee. PP*&*C is an innovative organization which raises money by publishing books of noted authors, representing all genres. Its face and voice is **David Russell Tullock** (dtullock@parsonsporch.com).

Parson's Porch *&* Company *turns books into bread & milk* by sharing its profits with the poor.

www.parsonsporch.com

Fertile Decay

CONTENTS

LIVING

DYING

THRIVING

Living

SECRET SELF

Oh my,
you are a slippery serpent, aren't you?
I can't quite get a grip on you.
It shouldn't be this way.
It should have been easy for us,
obvious,
clear as day,
natural, and pure.
I should have awakened to you
with celebration and freedom,
like dawn breaking.
But you were stifled,
sanitized, forbidden, and buried.
I only know the half of you,
the half that didn't make those around me
queasy.
But you are there,
more than what the eye can see.
I've always known,
but the permitted half
that saw the light of day
made it easy to conform
and lock you away.
I'm sorry.
It's not fair to you.
You are not the filthy creature
that the screamed lies
damned you to be.
You are beautiful and right.
But now,
I don't know how to hold you,
so you keep slipping away from me.

I hope there will come a day
in the glorious dawn
we were both denied,
when you and I can breathe in
the dewy fog of sunrise
in the light,
in full view,
together and whole.

CANDLE IN THE HALLWAY

As the time for sleep closes in
I lock the door,
switch off the lights,
and I am about to blow out the candle
in the hallway
when I pause.
All is quiet.
The flame does not make a sound,
but does make itself known.
The light and the dark
dance along the walls.
Often we think to preserve the glow
and fear what comes in shadow.
But this flickering waltz
reminds me that both light and dark
are equally beautiful
and good
in their own right.
The light reveals and guides,
like a lighthouse on a rocky cliff.
But the darkness provides rest and transformation
like a protective chrysalis.
Both are hopeful and helpful.
I huff out the flame
without any fear of the dark surrounding me.
It will renew me for when the light comes again.

THAT LADY

Bulky, cumbersome, loud,
large and empty,
an excellent receptacle for bags of trash,
regurgitating garbage on a regular basis,
permanently stained with a slimy film of filth,
reeking of rot;
for you, every day is trash pick up day.

WASTE OF TIME

People are obsessed with reminding you
that time passes quickly,
life is short,
you're always running out of moments.
And now I have a complex.
When hard work leads to failure
I agonize over the precious, fleeting time
that I have wasted.
I chastise myself over every wrong decision,
and I wring my hands wishing
I could go back and reclaim the moments
that were stolen
and led me to a dead end.
But this wastes even more time!
I cannot hate myself
for every mistake.
I cannot consider each wrong
to be a wrong.
Maybe we're the unforgiving ones,
and we can't face that harsh reality.
So we blame time instead.
If we are more generous with ourselves
maybe time will be too.

REGRET?

I don't know if I regret it.
Or if I should.
Or what I'll get out of it if I do.
Or if I don't.

FARMLAND

Weeds ripped up, stones tossed away.
Soil plowed through,
harrowed dry and unrecognizable.
The earth has been turned and scarred,
left fallow for this season.
No seeds, no sprigs and sprouts,
no green growth
on this bitter, brown bed.
It looks like a fresh grave.
Maybe it is.
But that doesn't mean that some time,
a little later down the road,
it won't be bursting to abundant life again.

WINDOWSILL

The cunning spider
always finds the windowsill
slightly cracked open.
She squeezes her body through
and spins her web.
I leave her be
to quietly trap pests.
I place the orchids
that I couldn't resist when at the market
on this windowsill
to bloom purple.
I wedge the feather I found in my yard
in the windowsill
to remind me to stay wild.
It is the earth's gift
to observe this ecosystem
on my windowsill.

COOKING I

Sometimes the sauce needs to simmer
for a little while
to melt the flavors
of garlic and tomatoes together.
Sometimes the meat needs to braise
for hours and hours
for the jus and herbs to harmonize.
Sometimes the stew needs to cook
low and slow
all the day long
for the vegetables to soften
and the broth to bolden.
Patience is the best recipe.

JUST SUMMER

I reached the forest at the edge of the clearing,
and my hands touched the bark of the willow tree.
The breeze shook her elegantly drooping branches
that gently stroked my hair.
I wanted to pitch my tent here
under her caring canopy.
But I heard a song in the air,
one that drew me away.
I had to follow it, just to see the source.
Something about the way the wind
sifted through the far off branches
enticed me.
I found him.
An old oak, with mighty branches
drooping low to the ground.
He was the one singing.
The song was nice,
but I wanted to return to my willow.
"Oh but don't go!"
cried the oak.
"Look how my branches hang so low,
so low they can kiss the earth.
I am grounded and strong,
I have been here for so long.
You can easily climb upon my branches,
and I will support you.
I am deeply rooted, so rooted that nothing can move me.
Here, climb on.
I have been disappointed time and time again
as people have passed me by."
I shifted on my feet. Unsure.
Maybe just try?

I climbed onto a heavy-laden branch.
This was pleasant,
but it was no willow.
I considered getting back down when the oak said,
"But look how close the next branch is!
You can keep climbing!
Imagine how far you will go,
how far I can take you."
How far you can take me?
I was doing all the work.
But going far, climbing high sounded awfully tempting.
Maybe the willow wouldn't be able to offer me that.
I climbed higher.
"Keep going, you will find fruit.
Apples, bananas, oranges,
all for you!
See what I can do for you?"
Strange,
oak trees don't grow that fruit.
But I could see up high the dangling color-shine.
I wanted something sweet.
So higher I went.
Grab, pull, step, stand.
I worked hard for what I wanted,
sweat glistening,
knowing the fruit would taste all the better once I earned it.
"Almost there!"
encouraged the old, rooted tree.
"See how I have helped you climb?"
But I was the one with splinters, scrapes, and blisters.
The tree's bark had scratched me to bits.
This was my labor, not his.
Finally, the dangling fruit was within reach!
I leaned as far as I could to grab the
seductive orange.

My fist closed,
squish.
My hand crushed the fruit,
and my fingers were coated in pungent slime.
Rotten fruit.
Stolen fruit.
The fruit did not belong to this tree.
I fell back against the trunk,
expecting support,
but the bark gave way to rot.
This ancient tree, rooted in the earth
covered in unearned fruit gone bad,
was rotten to the core.
The oak shook with laughter as I fell to the ground.
Twigs and leaves broke my fall before I landed
knocking the wind out of my lungs.
The oak laughed cruelly as I caught my breath.
I told the oak he was bad.
He was a lie.
"So? I have been here so long
that my roots have become one with the soil.
Nothing can move me!"
Ah yes.
The oak was right.
Nothing could move him.
But neither could he leave.
He had set his own trap.
Through his apathetic comfort
and sham of a legacy,
he was tall and proud,
but would soon collapse into his own rot
when the next storm came.
I got my breath, nursed my wounds.
I cast one more longing glance at the willow,
knowing it was too late to go back to her,

and then I moved on.
I walked away
because I could.
I had no roots trapping me.
I would be able to withstand
the thunder rumbling in the distance.

FERTILE DECAY

I'm ready.
It's time for a compost pile.
First come the eggshells
that I had to tiptoe on
so as not to offend you.
Then come the dry leaves
from the bushes I had to beat around
so that you never had to face the truth.
Next are the banana peels,
the traps of deceit
you laid down to slip me up.
After that, I dump in the clippings
that I had to cut down
to reveal your identity
as a snake in the grass.
Finally, I sprinkle in the ashes
from the letters and pictures
that I set aflame.
This pile is rotten,
reeking of death.
But my, oh my,
just wait and see
the life I will be able to grow
from this fertile decay.

VORACIOUS

I tried to skip a rock across the lake
but I didn't throw it quite right
so it didn't skim,
but got swallowed.
The lake swallowed the little rock right up.
Well, what else has this gluttonous beast
gulped down its gullet?
Branches? Entire trees?
Muddy banks?
Ducks, geese, swans?
Deer, raccoons, otters?
Boats? Swimmers?
Well, you won't be gorging on me!
Not today.
Besides, you would choke anyway.
The lake looks so deceptively placid,
but don't turn your back,
or the lapping shallows
will lap you up.

WISDOM I

I think that we've forgotten
about wisdom.
Knowledge is not the same
as wisdom.
Experience is not the same
as wisdom.
Age is not the same
as wisdom.
Wisdom is not about doling out
unnecessary, unasked for, unwanted advice
to boost your own ego.
Wisdom is not thinking
that you have all the answers.
Wisdom is not being the eldest in the room.
Wisdom is learning from your experience
and from the experience of others.
Wisdom is knowing what works for you
may not work for another.
Wisdom is allowing people to learn their own lessons.
Wisdom is admitting
that there is always, always, always
more to learn.
Wisdom is knowing that you will never
ever, ever
have all the answers.

MARSHLAND

The thunder cracks in the distance,
as I stand
hypnotized
at the edge of the marshland.
The screaming cicadas
and whipping wind
warn me to shelter soon,
but the water, rushes, and reeds
beckon me closer.
The great blue heron gracefully, urgently glides away
entreating me to do the same,
but I inch closer and closer.
What harm could one little step
into the wetland do?
Suddenly a great flash
that strikes too close for comfort
breaks the trance,
as it sears off a nearby branch.
I topple over into the rich, deep mud
that hugs me a little too tight.
I pull myself free
from the final attempt to suck me in
as a permanent member of the marsh.

MORE THAN A PILLAR

She who is the strongest
is also the most exhausted.
If you often find yourself leaning heavily
on her unyielding frame
consider what a relief it would be
if she herself did not have to be
so deeply rooted upright
and could lean in repose.
However, when you offer her rest,
she will decline.
So offer again,
and again,
and again.
It will take more than one invitation
for her to entertain the notion
that she is safe enough to relax.
She does not slumber
because she is accustomed to taking
first watch,
second watch, and third.
She knows that falling apart is a privilege.
Be patient, and have your arms out
ready to catch her descent,
but don't pull her in
unless she asks;
don't grab tight
unless she says so.
Be prepared, because it will be so heavy,
maybe unbearably so,
but bear it with her,
because her shoulders have sagged
under the weight of holding it on her own.

She has had to be
everything to everyone,
and she has told the world
that she has a high threshold for pain,
when she really just masks it well.
If there is silence,
let it be,
even if it stretches long.
When she is ready to stand
only help her up if she requests.
And now that you have her trust
stay on your toes.
She may need you sooner and more often,
but she will remain a bastion for you,
so long as you are for her.

CREAKING TREES

When the wind winds through
the naked branches of the trees
and the boughs stiffly sway,
creak, and groan
I do not think the forest is protesting
a disturbance.
The gust is a massage therapist
discovering the sore spots,
gently, carefully working them out
with nimble fingers.
For the trees
it hurts so good,
the needed touch
bringing both pain and relief.

A PLANET ALL MY OWN

Don't worry about me.
I'm going to float off to find
a planet all my own.
It can truly be disorienting
to travel untethered and adrift.
Sometimes I turn my longing eyes
back to the poisoned planet
where I at least could rely on the gravitational pull
to remind me where I belonged.
But having a place,
and being wanted
is not enough
to drag me back down
into an atmosphere determined to flood my lungs
with toxic, gaseous fumes.
I'll take my chances
with the cosmos to a destination unknown.
There is no map or compass or coordinates
to direct my floating body
to the planet that I should claim
for my new home.
So I will latch onto the closest asteroid,
riding the streak of uncertainty.

HAVEN

The trees in front of me
begin to sink in the flood.
Everything in my sight
is swallowed up
by the sting in my eyes.
And I just can't look at him.
Instead, I ask,
"Sometimes do you ever just…?"
The tears dribble down.
There's no stopping them now.
"Yes, all the time,"
he replies.
My head finds that tender bed
between his shoulder and collarbone
a haven to lay down
my weary, burdened mind.
All is not well,
but I am held.

DRAGON IN THE SKY

It's bittersweet to look up above
and see a cloud so obviously
shaped like a dragon
leaping across the sky.
The sweetness of childhood returns
when I could believe
that the cloud was a hint
that dragons were real
and if I just kept my eyes open
and wished hard enough
I would be worthy enough,
special enough
to glimpse one.
I would have knowledge
that no one else had.
I would be the chosen one.
The bitterness comes now that I have grown
knowing that I am in a world without
this fantasy magic.
I didn't find the dragon cave,
fairies never came to take me
on a midnight adventure,
I never saw a unicorn under the moonlight,
and mermaids didn't come swimming by.
I was never deemed chosen or special
by otherworldly creatures
who wanted me to be among them.
But I have come to love
the power of my imagination,
and my strength that has come
from surviving the unsurvivable.
I have become my own magic.

WADING

A sickening feeling sinks in,
seaweed has wrapped around my ankle.
Even worse,
I just stepped on some.
It squished between my toes
with a nauseating tickle.
I kick the seaweed away,
but I don't leave the water.
I don't jump anymore
when the seaweed assaults my feet.
I used to think some creature of the depths
had come to claim me,
but now I know
it is harmless.
Seaweed is not a threat.
Unpleasant, yes,
but not a watery doom.
I can shake it off,
and keep wading.

UNAGING

Ageless.
Isn't that what we all want to be?
Forever young?
But take a look at the hollowed-out log.
There it lies
with the inner wood carved away
without any rings left inside
to reveal how many years
that the tree might have lived.
Now it will never grow old;
but it will not grow anything at all,
no leaves, fruit, or buds.
It cannot stand
as the roots have withered and crumbled.
It is empty, lifeless,
and ageless.

CAN'T RETURN

I'm finding it difficult to admit
that there are pieces of me
that are gone
forever.
Certain parts
simply aren't coming back.
The same fire,
passion,
hopes,
and dreams
have disappeared for good.
I can't return to who I was.
But I can learn to love
who I am now.
Many of my old fears are gone
and this is liberating,
because I have conquered innumerable perils.
I have power and confidence
that most won't acquire in their lifetimes.
And then there are certain pieces
of who I have been
that has laid dormant,
slumbering deep inside,
waiting for the sunrise.
That dawn has come,
and those bits of my soul
are awakening, rubbing their eyes,
stretching long, and standing tall.
I cannot return,
but I can become
over and over again.

ARE YOU LISTENING?

Good God.
You're the one who wanted me here,
the one who demanded
I stand before you
and speak
like a trained animal.
I prepared for hours,
days,
years
to satisfy your standards.
I didn't just jump through regular hoops
for you,
they were riddled with poisoned tipped needles,
and both hands bound behind me.
And now that I am finally here,
you aren't listening to a word I say.
You may sit at attention,
nod,
take notes,
and even compliment my work.
But then you remain unmoved
and impossible.
I toppled every mountain
you erected before me
and you're unapologetically unbearable.
I can't keep showing up.
I won't.

Dying

VOID

I've heard some nonsense
about staring at the abyss,
and the abyss staring back.
Bullshit.
I dare the abyss to look me right in the eye.
I challenge the void to scream
right back at me.
Coward.

SKINNED ALIVE

Step lightly.
Mind your toes.
Yes, that's me,
the pile on the floor.
I'm a bundle of
exposed nerves
raw and volatile.
Be sure to skirt around me
with care
because any nudge,
jostle, or brush,
no matter how
unintentional
will result in
excruciation.
Just be patient,
and watch out for me
while my skin grows back.

MOLTED

There was a beetle husk
left molted on top of the gravestone.
It was hearty and in perfect shape.
It was certainly from a leaf beetle.
A cottonwood beetle?
Dogbane?
Or maybe a swamp milkweed?
It had died a kind of death
in solidarity with whoever lies beneath.
And then it walked out of its tomb,
shiny, fresh, and softened.
It crawled off to live another day,
leaving the skin
an offering to the deceased.

STARDUST

Let's nip this lie
right in the bud.
I have heard enough about trying to shoot for the moon,
and landing in the stars!
That's not how pursuing your dream works.
The moon is unattainable,
and the stars are laughing.
You can't depend on them to catch you.
If you land on one of them,
they'll toss you over their shoulder
and watch you land in the dirt.
They'll cackle as your bones crackle
and remind you that as you lay in the dust
you are also dust.
Not just any dust,
stardust.
They'll tell you that you are
only a pile of leftover star carcass.
Pick yourself up,
and don't trust the stars.

NOT TO BE DRAMATIC...

Would I be considered a
tortured soul?
No!
Obviously not.
That's fairly melodramatic,
awfully over-the-top,
don't you think?
It's just...
There's a dull, throbbing pang
that is always present
deep in some cavity
in my chest.
Even when things are just fine,
and I am going about my day
I know it's there
taking up space within me.
But a tortured soul?
That's a bit much.
That's only a phrase romantics use
for unrequited love.
I just have an insatiable yearning
for a better day
where it doesn't hurt to breathe.
If I stay up a little too late
I might sob a bit,
and shoot sharp questions like darts
to the universe,
to God,
to the voiceless dark.
But to call myself a tortured soul
would be attention-seeking
and self-serving indulgence.

I just wonder if it's possible
for a heart
to ache itself away.

ODE TO THE CHURCH

I suppose you thought
the bundle in your hands
was a bouquet of roses,
because you saw the thorns
and you assumed the blooms
had just fallen off.
Then, you thought that
with enough love and time,
the roses would blossom again.
I beg of you to look down,
and see that the growing red
is not a flower
but your own blood.
What you are clutching to
for dear life
are thistles.
They have buried themselves
so deeply in your palms
that your life is freely flowing from you.
But you will not look.
You would rather sacrifice your very soul
than break the blissful illusion.
Even as the thistles twist and tighten
around your wrists,
digging and slicing dangerously,
you will not release
what is killing you.
I tried, truly,
to reach out at my own peril to help you.
You screamed at me,
recoiled at my compassionate touch,
and my own hands were shredded to pieces.

Sometimes one must lose everything
to be saved.
But it seems as if it might be too late for that.
You will not break your grip,
and the thistles seem to have claimed you.
I see that you are weakening,
dying,
when you don't have to.
But I guess the prickles can only be pried
from your cold, dead hands.
You want to trap others in the thistles,
but they know better.
They won't come near,
and you don't understand why.
I cannot die with you,
even though you want to take me
and everyone you know
down, down, down.
I will walk away.
You will call me names.
You will feel betrayed.
You will think I am not good enough.
You will say I am the problem.
You will tell me I am taking the easy way out.
But today, I shall live.
With my scars, I shall live.

TRUST ARMS LIKE MINE

You can't see it,
but I can.
There's a snake in the grass over there.
I know the serpent appears to be
a trusted friend whose threatening hisses
are disguised as dulcet tones.
You don't want to believe that your slithering companion
who you've trusted
is rearing up to strike.
But before you walk toward the trap,
hear my plea
and just take a look at my arms.
Do you see the knotted scar tissue
twisting up them?
That's from the venom
that was mercilessly injected into me
from my own snake bites.
I am forever marred
by the fangs of presumed friends.
I survived,
but I want to spare you from the searing pain
and permanent reminders.
I know how to spot a snake in the grass.
These are arms you can trust.

AUDIENCE

Do you ever feel like
there is an audience watching your demise
from afar,
rooting for your failure,
hoping you burn out bright
and then fade into obscurity,
so much so that no one remembers
that you even exist?
Or even worse,
that there is an audience
who has been cheering you on
and invested so much in your potential,
but they get weary from watching you continually
stumble,
fall,
flop,
flounder,
and let them down,
proving them wrong for ever believing in you
in the first place?
Yeah, me neither.

COOKING II

The meat must be butchered,
chopped,
and sizzled.
The vegetables must be pulled,
picked,
and boiled.
The herbs must be clipped,
ripped,
and cooked.
Carnage is always a necessary ingredient.

WISDOM II

Wisdom comes with a high price tag.
Wisdom comes from the ache
of rarely getting the closure or answers
that you so desperately want.
Wisdom comes from justice denied.
Wisdom comes from normalized mistreatment.
Wisdom comes from trusting yourself,
loving yourself,
advocating for yourself,
when everyone around you is doing
otherwise.

HAUNTED ECHOES

I empty myself of all fear,
rage, guilt, stress,
grief, and anguish
as I scream into the canyon.
There is something satisfying
about my stinging eyes,
raw throat,
and echo bouncing
against the eroded-smooth walls.
But instead of my voice fading away,
it rushes back to me
like a boomerang.
I duck down and cover my ears
but my scream permeates my hands,
throttling my eardrums
and a burst of wind blows back my hair.
That wasn't as cathartic
as I had anticipated.
I cautiously stand surveying my surroundings,
and I decide that it is safe to walk away.
I stagger on,
with my echo haunting me
itching my ears,
tickling my brain.

COMING AND GOING

In each doorframe of the house
I took invisible ink
and wrote your name
coupled with a curse,
so that with every entrance and exit
you would be walking through
a maleficent web.
And now doom shall bite at the heels
of your comings and goings,
your foundation shall weaken
to a brittle state,
and your house will collapse in ruin.
You, who have escaped suffering
and had an easy existence,
you, who have garnered sympathy
while conducting sinister matters
behind closed doors,
you, in your twilight years,
will finally taste the harvest
of every poisoned seed you've sown.
The final chapter of your privileged,
unburdened life
will smolder in utter waste

EXTINGUISHED

It's scary in the cold and dark.
I've always had a fire
to light the path,
to fuel my dreams,
to fight off attacks,
to overcome obstacles.
When I had nothing,
I at least had my flame.
I was the fire,
a flame on the move.
Now there's not even
a leftover ember.
The charred wood has gone cold,
and now even the ashes
are spiraling off into the breeze.
I knew that I could lose everything.
I didn't know
that I could lose this.
I didn't know
this could be taken from me.
I know nothing.

FALSE SIGNS

Perhaps you are looking for a sign.
Aren't we all?
I'm going to offer you a warning.
You don't have to take it,
but I feel a responsibility to share
what I know.
Dreams are not always the sign you are looking for.
They are not always a prophecy
sent to you
at just the right time
to guide you on your quest.
Sometimes,
often times,
they are just dreams.
Your brain is trying to process
and file away
all of your experiences,
memories,
stresses,
hopes,
and fears.
Please keep that in mind.
Dreams aren't always a map
to point you in the right direction.
Do your discernment
in the daytime
when you are awake with some clarity.
Make sure you've eaten,
maybe had some coffee.
Talk to other people.
Look for a sign or an epiphany
in the daytime,

when you are in charge of your faculties.
Dreams that seem to give you an
"answer"
can lead you straight into
the snapping jaws of a predator.
Not a dream predator,
a real-life one.
I know you need a sign,
I get it.
Really.
But dreams might confuse your logic
and intuition.
Trust yourself,
not the prophecy fabricated
by your sleeping mind.

HOLLOW HALL

Pad, pad, pad,
gentle fall my feet
on the ever-rolling carpet
that streams down the hollow hall.
The doors lead to nowhere, no place,
no time.
The pictures in the frames reflect empty
with vague silhouettes
that only can be seen in the peripheral.
The mirrors silently crack,
soundless splinters threatening to burst.
The clocks are ominously motionless,
with hands jutting out in opposing directions.
The rusted key in my hand
is mated to one of these locks.
I am drawn by heat emanating
from the source I seek.
With trepidation, I steadily move in,
never breaking my pace or a sweat,
even as the heat rises dry.
The key tingles in my hand
as the feverish wave becomes unbearable.
The lock to my right burns white,
hanging on the wall as an ornamentation
with no door anywhere near.
I slide my vibrating key into the hole,
and click it to the right.
The floor shifts beneath me,
the rug rips,
and the floor paneling cracks open.
A door swings open a few yards down the hall.
Tripping and scrambling

over the shaking, breaking floor beneath me,
I clammer to the open door for my escape.
I close my eyes and leap,
unsure of how it will feel to launch
into a void,
but feet find firm, soft ground.
Pad, pad, pad,
go the sound my feet, knees, and hands
as I tumble inside.
Something clangs along the floor next to me.
The key?
No. A different one.
This one roughed with chipped paint.
I finally lift my head to observe my surroundings.
Another hollow hall.
For a brief moment I allow myself
to wallow,
but I swallow the rising bile down,
wrap my hand around the new key,
and accept my destiny
to be the keeper of hollow hall.

WITHERING PLACES

The soil is barren here.
My roots are shriveled shallow.
I topple over and break.
Do not weep for me,
because this is not my first life cycle
in withering places.

ODD ONE

There are places set at the table,
but I can't find a seat.
There are prepared plates of food,
but the kitchen is one short,
and I am last in line.
We are playing a game,
but the cards fold right as it gets to my turn.
I hear jokes and laughter,
but the crowd disperses when I arrive.
The applause runs out
when I take the stage.
I get the hint.

DISCIPLE

I sandaled my feet,
shouldered my cross,
I let the dead bury the dead,
and I faithfully followed you.
I put in the miles,
sacrificed time, money, and dreams,
I served with my hands and feet,
I laid down my pride,
I tossed aside my own needs and desires,
believing it would all be worth it.
But I suffered and suffered
without any relief in sight.
I was hated like you said I would be,
but you didn't help me.
You didn't send back up.
When it got hard,
you fled the scene,
taking everyone else with you
and I got crushed under the cross.
I wasn't looking for glory,
but I also didn't plan on
dying and descending into hell
every single day
without any resurrection
to help me back up.

COSMIC BALANCE

I wish I could believe in balance,
that good and bad find a way
to be held together
in tension.
I wish there was really a cosmic correction
when the crushing weight
of devastation knocks you right off
the great scale of existence.
I wish that when a series of bad things happens
that meant for sure
that a parade of goodness
would come marching around the corner
with fanfare and confetti.
I wish I could believe that all shall be well,
that everything will be okay,
that you reap what you sow,
that it will all work itself out in the end.
But those of us
who have walked with
the companion of suffering
know the truth.
We are hardened
from saving ourselves
because the universe has no plan
to save us.
There is no balance,
only grit.

FUNERAL

How many times have I died now?
I've lost count.
And who are these people who line up
out the door
to lay flowers on me?
Did they come out of the woodwork
just for this?
Where were they before?
I don't even recognize
a good number of these faces.
Now they are saying nice words.
Where were these words
when I was breathing?
It is easier for people to visit my grave
than to visit my home.

LOCKED

Despair is the darkest of places.
There is no light to look toward.
Maybe you will lie there for a while,
enrobed in pitch black.
But perhaps you'll reach out.
Perhaps your fingers will graze
another hand desperately grasping for yours.
Fingers lock.
Strangers,
bound in starless night,
but not alone.

Thriving

WHEN THE WORLD IS BLUE

All is quiet.
Few stir.
The hot has steamed cool.
And for a moment
the world is blue.
When the sun has set,
but the stars aren't quite ready to twinkle,
I am in the center
of this blue bubble.
My focus is soft,
no thing demanding my attention.
I am free to float
in this aquarium.
Suspended.
POP.
The sudden shimmer of stars
bursts the bubble blue.
The blanket of night towels me dry,
and the sandy stars stick to my feet.
In the dark
I'm still baptized in blue.

SPRING PEEPERS

The spring showers created little puddles
in the dirt around the gravel driveway.
These tiny pockets of water
teemed with life
as the little tadpoles took their first swim.
I'm hidden away in a spacious hollow
without any homes near mine.
No one is here to visit me,
but there is no one here to betray me either.
However, these tadpoles were pleasant company.
I spent the weeks
ensuring the pools remain hydrated
for my new neighbors.
Sometimes they zoomed across the puddle,
other times they lolled about.
I reached out, dipped my fingertip in the water
and tried to touch one.
They were quick to escape.
I wasn't offended,
I understood the need to recoil.
Soon the tadpoles sprouted legs,
then became little Spring Peepers
that hopped away from me.
At first, I thought they had betrayed me, too.
But now I know that the song they sing me each night
is their gratitude for being a friend
but respecting their space.

PERMISSION

I give myself permission
to be too much,
to have a strong personality,
and to not be liked by everyone.
I can learn more
and be better
and forgive others
and I can apologize when I hurt,
but I cannot manage everyone else's emotions
for them.
I am responsible for myself,
my actions, my choices,
and responsible for doing the least amount of harm,
but I do not need to be
a people pleaser
who must check off every standard
others expect of me
to earn their friendship.
I am not customizable.
I give myself permission
to appreciate myself
when others do not.
I give myself permission
to befriend my own soul.

VISITORS

Sweet little tree frog,
thank you for picking my front porch
to lounge this afternoon.
I hope you feel safe here.
Please feel free to sing me a tune
if you feel so inclined.
But if you'd rather nap,
then sleep in peace.
Oh my, baby raccoon,
what a ferocious cry you have!
Do you hear that?
Mama's not far away,
she's looking for you too.
She's trotting to you
with all your little siblings.
Thank you for letting me
witness your family reunion.
Have a safe trip home.
Hello, young miss doe,
I see that you are on an adventure all your own
dining on a fresh salad in my backyard.
Thank you for having dinner with me tonight.
I hear you rustling in the brush
just outside, little fox.
I know you noticed the rabbits nearby
and that's why you're here to visit.
I won't harm you,
I just want to sneak a peek.
Thank you for pausing
just under the street light
and looking me right in the eye
allowing us to acknowledge each other.

Dearest family of cardinals,
a half dozen it seems,
thank you for choosing the bushes
directly outside my kitchen window
to flit to and fro
to chase and to bask.
You brighten up the winter-dead foliage
with your carefree crimson.

NEIGHBORHOODS

Solitude can be healing,
but I cannot deny the comfort
that neighborhood sounds and smells bring me.
Neighbors chatting on their front porches
laughing at jokes that I can't quite make out.
Simply being humor adjacent
still makes me smile.
The musk of a bonfire
sifting through my backyard
gives me warmth,
even if I can only see and smell the smoke.
The sound of dogs barking
and children playing
reminds me of the innocence still left
in a ravaged world.
The fragrant rose bush from a nearby yard
proves that there are still people
who turn the soil
and patiently care for the earth.
The squeal of the brakes
from the school bus,
from the garbage collectors,
and from the mail carrier
shows me that we all have a role
in the community,
and we depend upon one another.
We are living our individual lives
but we are connected.

RIPPLES

You never know what gifts the ripples
will carry to shore.
A golden leaf could float by,
a floating insect might come skimming,
dancing across the surface,
or a bottle could bob along the ripples
with a message inside.
This would be a rare opportunity.
I suggest you pop the cork
and unfurl the parchment
earnestly, tenderly.
The writer of this letter probably passed into eternity
a little while ago,
but for just a moment two timelines converged
and they are alive
and you are alive.
Don't share these words with anyone
or you will break the spell of time travel.
Instead, pen your own words,
roll them up tight,
and cork them away.
Trust the waters to hold your time capsule
and deliver it through the ripples
so that you may defy the spinning of the world again.

TRAINS

So long as I can hear
a train horn blare
echoing nearby
I know that I haven't strayed too far.
A train regularly rattled
my childhood home,
and I'd race to the window
enthralled to wave it by.
Another blazed by at midnight
while I was studying in college,
reminding me that I was not the only one
awake late, toiling away.
When I moved out of state
and felt homesick,
the late-night train found me
and whistled to me that I wasn't lost.
Now, as I settle on a new patch of land,
one I'd like to keep for a while,
the train that cuts through downtown
tells me that this is a comely site
to sink some roots.

POCKETS

The elderly church folk
may be stubborn
about which pew belongs to them,
but they are generous
with what's tucked away in their pockets.
If you're in need of waded up tissues
they have plenty to spare.
When you're searching for a pen
they have enough for you to choose
your preferred color of ink.
They've got lozenges for coughs,
mint gum for your breath,
and butterscotches for the little ones.
You might even be lucky enough
to get a toothpick
when the Sunday potluck
gets stuck in your teeth.
Blessings abound
from the pockets of
Betty Jo, Alberta, Jerry,
Jimmy, Phyllis, and Reginald.

EMPTY LIBRARY

What happens when you realize
that you're all alone among the ever-spanning rows
of shelves
packed with stacks of books?
Each turn of the corner
a mystery,
a pit in your stomach as you expect to find a stranger
but enter the row to find
no one.
Is it more unsettling to know that
someone is watching,
or that no one is?
There is a magic in the suspense
as you have the freedom to explore the titles
of thriller, mystery, sci-fi, and fantasy.
You are alone in a world of worlds,
living in a delicious secret,
afraid of getting caught,
but also titillated at the possibility.

THE WORLD'S A FEAST

My hungry eyes gaze at tempting Tuscany.
My stomach growls at the thought of appetizing Aukland.
So I begin simmering the stew of Katmandu,
basting a baking Bangalore,
and jovially munching on Munich.
I lose control and swallow Seoul whole,
I'm taking my time and sucking the marrow out of Moscow,
I notice Nice stuck in my teeth.
For dessert, I spy the stiff meringue peaks of Everest and
Kilimanjaro.
I've got an insatiable hunger for a kingdom,
I'm feasting piece by piece.
Please, come to the table
and share this meal with me.

CITY LIGHTS

I'm still a bit of an amateur
when it comes to city living.
Rural countryside and small cities
are my custom.
These hold rustic charm
and quaint beauty,
but also have a lonely population.
Sleepy towns slow me down.
The big city may have suffocating crowds,
but the soaring towers
with lights that don't dim
remind me that the streets are alive
with possibility;
and that when I am awake
a little too late,
I'm not the only one
with eyes wide open.

COOKING III

You have some rice left over,
and I have some veggies
fresh from this morning's market.
She has tuna salad and stir fry,
he has some stray eggs.
What else is there to do
on a lazy Saturday
at noonday
when the world is cold outside
than take the ingredients
and the friends
that fate has blessed us with
and make a memory-meal?
There will never be another day
with these exact people
and this precise menu
in this specific place
ever again.
So eat of this food
and drink in this moment
before it passes us by.

WISHING WELL

Staring deep into the well,
I lazily wonder
if the coin weighing in my hand
is worth disturbing the still water beneath.
Which part of this equation
actually grants the wish?
The coin,
the water,
the action of tossing,
the splash,
the sinking to the bottom?
I roll the coin between my fingers,
then dangle it precariously over the stone walls
of the shadowed well
where I can't even see the bottom.
Dare I?
I pocket the coin
and drag my feet away,
yawning widely,
smiling dreamily.
I close my eyes
and make the wish anyway.

EYE CONTACT

My eyes are green some days,
blue on others.
Once you decide what color they are,
keep looking
and see what you might learn.
The well is deep,
allow yourself to fall.
You'll probably see a wearied soul.
You'll see a person
that's known abuse and abandonment,
and the prize of wisdom
won from suffering.
You'll probably see an age
that doesn't quite match the face.
You'll also find an empathy
that refuses to be suffocated
despite the mightiest of efforts
from the hands of an unforgiving world.
What you do with this knowledge is up to you.
You can acknowledge my journey
and respect my resolve.
Or you can dismiss it all,
crawl out of the well,
only recognize my superficial characteristics
of youth and womanhood,
and continue to believe that I am naive
and helpless.
But you cannot unlearn,
you cannot unsee.

FIELD OF PEACE

The Christmas lights have been
put away weeks ago.
The winter solstice rolls on
and on and on.
The night tumbles over the land
so early,
and the darkness billows,
obscuring the lake,
the homes, the trees, and the sky.
Driving home I feel alone
in the darkness flood.
But I know,
just a few miles from home
when my journey is coming to an end,
that there is a field
where the light is there to cheer me
on the final stretch.
A large string of lights
on the dried grass of the field
are draped in a circle
with the middle filled in
with a symbol of peace.
A peace sign that has outlasted
the other holiday lights
glows soft to warm the spirit
of all who drive by
or fly overhead.
Heavy eyes and weary body
are enlivened in the flowing waves of night.

CAN YOU HEAR IT?

The hymns we sang on Sunday morning,
that is the tune
that will lead me home.
My husband composing a new piece,
that is the tune
that will lead me home.
The songs I cried to in my teen years,
that is the tune
that will lead me home.
The tracks I played while I studied and dreamed,
that is the tune
that will lead me home.
The music my sister and I listened to in secret,
that is the tune
that will lead me home.
The songs I fell asleep to when I fought insomnia,
that is the tune
that will lead me home.
The musical numbers I learned for performance,
That is the tune
that will lead me home.
The lyrics I sing to soothe myself when I am afraid,
that is the tune
that will lead me home.
The song of this life that has yet to be completed,
that is the tune
that will lead me home.

NESTS

Have you ever wondered
how many strands of your hair
that have fallen to the earth,
have been plucked up by a songbird,
and woven into twigs
to make a nest?
Do you consider
how many homes
you are a part of
that keep little eggs warm,
and hug tight
cheeping babes?

WISDOM III

If your wisdom is verbose,
and neglects intentional silence
even when you're dying to speak,
then you do not have
wisdom.
Wisdom knows that people usually
aren't searching for words,
but a pair of ears.

WARMTH

The heart-shaped ornament
stuffed with dried lavender
never loses its scent,
year after year.
I remember France,
my first time overseas,
an adventure of youth
and the fragrance makes me feel
warm.
I sprinkle a little extra cinnamon
into the recipe
to add a punch of flavor.
I remember baking
for each holiday season,
stirring sweets together,
and licking the bowl.
The aroma is
warm.
The steaming mug of coffee
fogs up my glasses.
I remember long library evenings
studying,
writing,
and being anything but quiet.
The smell of the brew is
warm.
I burn some incense
to perfume my home,
the smoke rising and tickling my nose.
I remember being home-bound by snow
newly-wed and giddy,
pleased to be stuck inside

with the one I love most.
The spicy redolence burning
warm.

TONG SUNG KIDO

I am the foreigner here.
I look strange,
I do not speak the common tongue.
But the crowd looks on me with kindness.
And then together
they cry out loud
praying a prayer for me.
They've never seen me before today,
and I may never encounter them again.
And yet
their passion rings the rafters
as each person
pleads with God
on my behalf.
I cannot understand the words of the petitions,
but I comprehend the earnest energy
encompassing each spoken appeal.
Stranger am I
still cared for as familiar.

MINIATURES

I'm not sure why I have an affinity
for miniatures.
Tiny animals, furniture,
people, produce, clothing
that all fit between my fingertips
captivate me.
Perhaps it's the intricate details
or the delicate features
that hold me spellbound.
But it's more likely that
when I tenderly grasp the small figures
and turn them over
examining them gently
I consider how mighty I am
to these.
I could easily destroy this
still-life creation.
There would not be a loss of life,
but it would be a tragedy still
to abuse a small beauty.
It is my responsibility
to honor this fragile art.
The sacred art of life
is infinitely more complicated
than that of the voiceless,
thoughtless,
emotionless,
opinionless figurine.
But if we touched the living
more lightly
with just the brush of fingertips
we might captivate each other too.

ACKNOWLEDGEMENTS:

A special thank you to the Tupelo Press 30/30 Project for
publishing these poems:

A Planet All My Own
Audience
Candle in the Hallway
Dragon in the Sky
False Signs
Fertile Decay
Haunted Echoes
Molted
Neighborhoods
Nests
Ripples
Secret Self
Skinned Alive
Stardust
Unaging
Voracious
Warmth
Window Sill
Wishing Well
Withering Places